WHY
DID HE
DIE

SEVEN GREAT PURPOSES
IN THE PASSION OF GOD'S SON

James F. Fitzgerald

WatchWORD PRODUCTIONS
Pittsburgh, Pennsylvania

WHY DID HE DIE
Published by WatchWORD Productions

© 2004 by James F. Fitzgerald
International Standard Book Number (ISBN): 1-57466-111-6

Cover design by Mary Anne Skeba
Layout by Janet E. Dibble

Scripture quotations are from the following translations:

The Holy Bible, New King James Version
© 1984 by Thomas Nelson, Inc.

The Holy Bible, Contemporary English Version
© 1995 by American Bible Society

The Holy Bible, New International Version
© 1973, 1978 by International Bible Society,
used by permission of Zondervan Publishing House

For information:
WatchWORD Productions
Post Office Box 23300
Pittsburgh, PA 15222

CONTENTS

In memory of a great friend, Robert C. Crock, rejoicing in Paradise with our Lord Jesus. I give special thanks for the preaching of the Rev. John Guest that inspired the writing of this book. I'm also grateful to Carol Lee Neuman, Janet E. Dibble and Mary Anne Skeba for all their help in getting this book ready for publication, and to my remarkable wife and partner in life, Betty Fitzgerald, whom I dearly love.

ॐ

Personal Testimony

"...I shall fear no evil for thou art with me."
Psalm 23:4

I WAS TEN WHEN GOD first became real to me. That year, my mother, younger brother and I started attending church on Sunday mornings with my new stepfather. We had just moved from Chicago to a little town along the Ohio River outside of Pittsburgh where he'd been offered a teaching job.

What high hopes we had for our life together as a new family! But these hopes were soon dashed. One night when my mother was out, my stepfather acted inappropriately with me and made me promise not to tell. I didn't tell, but the next day I begged my mother never to leave me alone with him again. Not long after, they divorced, though I didn't understand why at the time.

Still, the three of us joined the Episcopal Church where he had taken us. There on Sundays I felt an incredible peace that was so different from what I felt anywhere else during the week.

Unlike the rest of my fifth-grade friends, I looked forward to church and took what I was learning about God seriously. At the same time, I could understand why they didn't much believe in him. They were just kids in a small town, I thought, kids who had never experienced the turmoil and trouble we had in my family.

Countless times as I grew up I remember walking home in the dark from a friend's, a sports event or youth group, and I sensed God's palpable presence with me. I couldn't go to sleep at night without first praying for the safety of all my relatives and special friends by name. Twice when my mother's life was in danger, God helped me to find her and save her life.

The summer after my junior year of high school, our pastor gave a sermon about not burying your talents. His message had an enormous impact upon me. Planning to pursue veterinary medicine in college, I took his words to mean I should develop my talent for creative writing instead.

A year later I left for college with a sincere faith in God and without much biblical knowledge. But by the end of those four years, I'd become a proud, out-spoken, atheist existentialist. I felt I needed these qualities to become a "great American novelist." I'd long since stopped praying.

But at age twenty six, I came to a sudden, deep, personal crisis. I'd already devoted five years' work to a single unfinished novel. It was my life. But what if I never completed it? I wondered. What if I just drifted off into oblivion? Was I crazy? What would become of me?

On the third day of my mental and emotional paralysis, God reached out to me in a remarkable way. It happened to be Ash Wednesday. An older waitress where I delivered beer called me over and smudged a dab of ashes on my forehead. As I walked away from her, I wondered if perhaps there really was a God. If he existed, maybe he would help me.

I decided to seek for God by laying aside my writing forty days. I'd been encouraged to see that I would start writing again on Monday, April 23, the birthday of my hero Shakespeare, a most auspicious date to me, and my "lucky number."

Later that night, filled with anxiety, the thought of dying without accomplishing anything terrified me. As I changed the radio station, by happenstance, the first voice that I heard said: "Commit your life to Christ! Commit your life to Christ! Commit your life to Christ!"

I stopped right where I was. I could hardly remember anything about who Christ was. What if I did follow him? Where would it lead me? In my mind I pictured walking through a maze. At that moment, I didn't even recall Christ's crucifixion or resurrection.

But I realized if I did stop writing, it didn't really matter what people might think of me. Nobody *truly* cared anyway. I was also convinced that the world would certainly self-destruct within a hundred years, so what was the point of writing for posterity either—if there would be none.

Suddenly a promise popped into mind that I hadn't heard since I was a boy: "Yea though I walk through the valley of the shadow of death, I shall fear no evil for thou art with me."

"Thou art with me!" The words were from a Psalm.

In a flash I recalled a number, Psalm 23, the same as my "lucky number," the date I'd start writing again. This must be a sign to me! God existed! He must care for me! He would help me!

Instantly, I understood that if this were true, my life had a purpose after all, and though I didn't know for sure what it was, an unexpected peace settled over me.

Everyday after that for the next forty days, something happened to convince me of God's reality. Again and again, I saw "providence in the fall of a sparrow."

On Easter Sunday, with a pony tail and in my work clothes, I went to church for the first time in years. I was humbled by all that I heard and had forgotten in my arrogant ambition.

It's been more than thirty years since God revealed himself to me that night over the radio station. Ever since, I've had an insatiable desire to learn all I could about this God who loved me and to share what I've learned with others. He's the reason for this book.

1

WHY DID HE DIE:
GOD'S PROMISE

*"Jesus then explained everything written about himself
in the Scriptures, beginning with the Law of Moses
and the Books of the Prophets."*
Luke 24:27

MY SUDDEN SPIRITUAL AWAKENING shook me to the core.
How could I write my book if I didn't know what God
had to say in his book? I should read the Bible first.

In my new zeal I made three vows: first to throw
away my years of writing, because I could now see that
my motives for writing the book were entirely selfish
and wrong. The years of work filled a large garbage can.

The second was not to start another book until I
had first read the Bible. I began reading it straight
through from Genesis. With the new activities and service I soon found myself involved in, that took two years.

Attending church again every Sunday, I also heard
the Bible read and taught. I was amazed at what it said.
Here I was a writer, and I'd never read more than a page
or two of this book. I went to Bible studies whenever I
could to absorb as much as possible. I had an intense
hunger to learn more about God.

But gradually I became frustrated that so much of
what I learned had little direction or cohesion. Mostly, I

studied disconnected Bible stories. I couldn't see the forest for the trees. To learn more, I took a graduate level tutorial; however, it did little to help me.

Since then, I've read the Bible through many times and studied it on my own, in seminary classes, courses and church. Over time, by God's grace, I came to a better understanding.

Actually, the Bible is a small library of 66 books. A variety of types of literature, from history and narrative to poetry, teaching and prophecy, fill its pages.

However, the Bible is anything but a disparate collection of loosely related writings about God. One principal truth shines out at the heart of understanding his Word. Yet, this truth is hardly taught.

The Bible is the true story of how God has worked in human history to fulfill a single remarkable promise he made in the Garden of Eden after the fall. Ultimately, nothing in the whole book is extraneous to the one great object of telling this story.

Composed over a period of fifteen centuries by nearly forty different authors working under the inspiration of the Holy Spirit, such single-minded purpose gives the Bible an incredible unity and reveals its divine authority like nothing else ever written.

———◈◈◈———

In sending his only Son to be executed upon a Roman cross, God accomplished great and eternal purposes planned before the creation of the universe. This book explores seven of the greatest of these purposes. The first is simply that God is the great God who keeps his word—for he had promised "The Passion of the Christ" from the beginning.

CREATION

The most famous sentence in all literature sets the stage brilliantly: "In the beginning God created the heavens and the earth" (Gen. 1:1). One short simple sentence introduces us at the beginning of space and time to the person of God the Creator, and to everything he created: that is everything existing apart from himself, visible or invisible.

Revealed in nature and scripture to be immortal and to possess a perfect character and almighty power, this invisible God crowned creation with the human race: made in his own spiritual image to be the apex of his creation. At each stage of his work, God, who cannot lie and who is never wrong, had assessed his creation, and said it was "good." "Good" in every sense of the word and in the highest sense of the word.

Upon finishing the work of creation, God rested on the seventh day and said of all he had made that it was "very good." Not good only, not good merely, but "good" in the superlative. If we had any doubt or question, God wanted us to know with certainty that his creation at the beginning was "good" indeed!

Here then, in such an amazing and remarkable environment, our first ancestors lived and moved and had their being. They found themselves fully formed in a garden of the greatest perfection earth has ever known. Here "Adam and Eve" were given dominion over all God had made.

And here God placed them on probation. He would test their obedience.

Two trees grew in the middle of the Garden of Eden (Gen. 2:9-17). One, the Tree of Life, held the promise of life everlasting. Of the other, the Tree of the Knowledge of Good and Evil, God commanded them not to eat. "For when you eat of it," God said, "you will surely die." The fruit of this tree alone remained off limits to them. Everything else in the garden was theirs to enjoy.

In the starkest of contrasts, the choice of eternal life and eternal death stood before them.

THE FALL OF THE HUMAN RACE

As the story goes, the serpent in the garden, possessed by Satan, tempted the woman to eat the fruit of the forbidden tree. Adam followed suit. The terrible consequence of this disobedience to God's clear command was that they fell immediately from their state of perfect innocence.

Instantly, their eyes were opened to this tragically changed condition. Overcome by guilt and fear, Adam and Eve hid from God when he came to question what they had done. Their relationship with their Maker had been altered forever.

By listening to Satan and rejecting God's will, in what

seemed to be a trivial act of disobedience, this couple, the fountainhead of the human race, had irreparably damaged themselves, their future progeny, the entire creation, and most of all, their relationship with God.

In the fall of Adam and Eve, as the Bible later reveals, three evil powers gained complete and total mastery over the human race: Satan, sin and death. Each power alone was more powerful than any human being. Apart from divine intervention, this trinity of evil powers now made the human condition utterly hopeless.

For their crime, Adam and Eve surely expected to be put to death immediately by their Creator. But in dispensing judgment, God remembered mercy. Instead of taking their lives, he gave them a promise of the greatest and most unexpected hope.

This promise helped them bear his judgment. Though Adam and Eve would continue living, she would suffer pain in childbirth and her husband would have dominion over her. The man would make his living by the sweat of his brow and all creation would resist him and no longer work easily with him. They'd be driven permanently from the Garden God had made for them, and eventually they would die, returning to the dust from which they'd come.

But before declaring these grievous pronouncements God directed his wrath upon the serpent. God sentenced this creature (and Satan behind it) to eventual destruction. Yet, in so doing, he pronounced his remarkable promise.

The Promise

God's great promise of deliverance is found in Genesis 3:15. It was given at the dawn of human history in the sparest of words.

God declared to the serpent that he would put perpetual enmity between it and the woman, and between its "seed" and her "seed." Furthermore, her male offspring would "crush his head," though the serpent would only bruise "his heel."

Recorded by Moses nearly thirty-three centuries ago, this obscure promise captured the essence of the Gospel message—the means by which God would save lost sinners. In figurative language, it proclaimed the coming of Christ and his mission. Jesus would be the male offspring who would crush the head of the serpent, even as he would be wounded

In a divine riddle, God revealed three amazing things about the Christ to come.

First, in its veiled words, lay hidden the incarnation of the sinless Son of God.

As we're told, a "*he*," the male offspring of a woman, would come in the future to crush Satan's head. Yet how could this ever be? Now that sin had entered the human race, every child of Adam must henceforth be subject by nature to the greater powers of Satan, sin and death.

However, the one to come was specifically called the "seed" of the woman. In careful terms, no mention was made of the seed of man. God's promise alluded to the virgin birth. The one to come would be conceived by the power of the Holy Spirit without the agency of man so as not to inherit a fallen human nature. Jesus would therefore not be subject to sin, Satan or death.

God's promise foretold a miracle. The incarnation was miraculous. The sinless Son of God was fully human without a fallen nature through his mother, and fully divine through the Holy Spirit. How else could he overcome the powers of darkness and redeem God's people?

Second, God's promise looked forward to Christ's crucifixion for sin.

It revealed that in his struggle with the evil one, the son of the woman would suffer. The evil serpent would bruise or "strike his heel." Yet, though this holy one must suffer through no fault of his own, the striking of his heel foretold a wound not mortal to God's immortal Son.

And so it happened. In a few precious words, God's promise foresaw Christ's holy passion as a sacrifice for sin. Jesus Christ was cruelly beaten and mocked at his trial. A spike was driven through his heel in crucifixion. On the cross he died for sin. But this was not the end.

Third, in cryptic words, God's promise foretold Christ's victory over the three great enemies of the human race: Satan, sin and death.

While "his heel" would be bruised in battle, *he* would "crush" the serpent's head. The crushing of his head meant a mortal blow to the devil. In other words, the offspring of the woman would destroy powerful Satan— the greatest power under God himself! (What torment this promise of destruction caused the devil from the day he heard it! One day, the son of the woman would defeat him!)

Furthermore, the one to come would be no sinner, or else he himself must also be a servant of sin and therefore Satan. But he would defeat the devil and must therefore defeat sin as well.

And though given to mortal combat with the evil one, the woman's seed would live. Yet Christ did die, but death could not hold him. The seed of the woman was immortal. Jesus Christ rose from the dead, resurrected on the third day.

In a puzzle, God had pledged a Deliverer to the founders of the human race. In promising victory to the woman's seed over Satan, sin and death, he gave hope to her descendents over the powers of darkness, too.

What a great and glorious promise God had given Adam and Eve in the face of absolute despair. Having brought destruction, sin and death into the world, they had obtained assurance of a Deliverer. Who but God could make such a promise? Who but Christ could accomplish it?

The rest of the Bible tells the story of how God worked to faithfully fulfill this amazing and gracious promise to send a redeemer to our race. Unfolding slowly through the millennia, God's plan was revealed with ever greater clarity until the coming of Christ in "the fullness of the time."

The fulfillment of this miraculous promise in the Garden is the inspired true story of the Bible.

FROM ADAM TO ABRAHAM *(GEN. 4:1-12:1)*

Countless times during the rest of their long, tedious lives, Adam and Eve found sole comfort in God's promise. Surely, Eve had hoped in her mother's heart that her first born son Cain would be the one God promised. Or perhaps it would be her second born, Abel. But Cain murdered Abel. Cain was not righteous and Abel, the first to die, didn't rise again.

Such experience certainly tempted the first two parents to question fallen woman ever bearing a son to overcome the evil powers afflicting the human race due to their sin. But God had promised. He alone could deliver them from the powers of darkness, sin and death.

Infected by evil as they were, the descendants of Adam and Eve continued to multiply upon the earth. As they populated the planet, the human condition rapidly degenerated. The world grew evermore corrupt and wicked.

Finally, seeing all the evil committed by his creatures, God declared he was sorry he'd created the human race. He determined to destroy life on earth in a great cataclysmic flood.

However, there was an exception. A man named Noah and his family. This one man found favor in the eyes of the Lord and was preserved along with his family and the creatures on the ark. A man of faith, Noah believed in God's gracious promise to his ancestors. We know this to be true because Noah pleased God, and without faith, it's impossible to please him (Heb. 11:6).

So much more than a children's story, the flood account is crucial to the fulfillment of God's great promise of redemption. In preserving Noah, God preserved his promise before two human witnesses to send a deliverer. If Noah and all his family had drowned with the rest of the world, the complete line of Adam and Eve would have been destroyed. The descendent of Eve whom he had promised could never come. In that case, God would have been broken his promise.

Of course, it's impossible for God to break his word—he is God! Therefore, for his promise to endure, he insured that at least one human couple continue the race. That one was Noah and his wife, with their three sons and their wives. Noah and his wife, you might say, were the neck of the funnel through which God's promise passed on its way to the coming of Christ.

After the flood, Noah's children alone were left to repopulate the earth. Shem, Ham and Japheth had children who had children and the race increased. But nothing much had changed.

Human nature was so corrupt not even the threat and experience of total destruction could change fallen humanity. This awful truth is meant to be one of the great lessons of the flood account. As God would have us fully understand, our only hope for deliverance lay in his promise.

Soon after, the people refused God's command to spread across the earth. At Babel, they banded together to build a tower to the heavens (could their motive be to protect against another flood?). But God intervened by confusing their language. Forced to stop building, the people scattered abroad, forming thereby all the future races and peoples of the world.

Amidst all this human confusion, God slowly and deliberately furthered his purpose of bringing the promised one into the world. Of Noah's three sons, Shem's line was chosen. Shem was father of the Semitic peoples.

FROM ABRAHAM TO MOSES (GEN. 12:1– EX. 18:27)

It was eight long generations after the flood before God called a Semitic man named Abram. This man was born in Ur, in the land of Mesopotamia, a place south of ancient Babylon, in the current country of Iraq. God called him to leave his country and kinsmen to go to a land that the Lord would show him. Possessed at that time by the Canaanites, it was the land of modern day Israel. In this place, through Abram, God would now prepare the way for "the line of promise."

When God called him, Abram was an older man and still childless. Yet God promised to make of him a great nation, and through him, to bless all the peoples on earth. Believing God, Abram traveled to "the land of promise" with his family and all his possessions (Heb. 9:11).

There in Canaan God established the covenant of circumcision, commanding Abram to walk blamelessly before him, promising greatly to increase his numbers. To confirm his promise, God changed Abram's name to Abraham, meaning "father of many nations" (Gen. 4:17).

In Canaan, Abraham had two sons. The first, named Ishmael, father of the Arab peoples, was born of a servant girl. Years later, the other, named Isaac, was born by his barren wife Sarah when she was too old to conceive.

Isaac then became the first born of the Jewish race. Isaac was the great miracle child of God's promise. Through him the Lord would continue his great purpose to bless all the peoples on earth by the coming of the promised Redeemer.

Isaac had two sons: Esau and Jacob. The younger, Jacob, was the one through whom God's promise would continue. Jacob had twelve sons and God changed Jacob's name to Israel, the name by which his descendants would be called.

In Abraham, Isaac and Jacob, we have the three great patriarchs of this Jewish nation (Ps. 105:9-10). Through them God began and prepared a unique people to record and preserve his commandments and oracles, and to be the people of the Messiah when he entered into our lost and dying world. The biblical history of the Jews is important because it's the history of the coming of the Messiah into the world: as Jesus told the Samaritan woman, "salvation is of the Jews" (Jn. 4:22b).

As Genesis records, Jacob went with his eleven sons and their families to Egypt to be with his son Joseph and to escape the seven years of famine. Generations passed in Egypt and the "Israelites" fell eventually into bondage as God had foretold Abraham centuries before.

No longer a small family, their numbers had increased so greatly they were now "a people" and a perceived threat.

To deliver the people of Israel, God raised up one of their own in the house of Pharaoh. Through Moses, God established the Passover and worked mighty miracles as Moses led God's "chosen people" out of Egypt into the wilderness to form a new nation.

FROM MOSES TO CHRIST (EX. 19:1 – MATT. 1:17)

At Mount Sinai, the Lord established Israel as a nation with Moses as their leader. He gave Moses the Ten Commandments carved in stone by his own hand as the Law they were to live by. God made a special covenant of blessing and cursing with Israel and promised to bless them if they kept his Law and to curse them if they failed to obey it.

As God directed him, Moses established the Tabernacle worship with the Priests and the Levites as their helpers. God instituted the system of animal sacrifices and offerings to atone for the sins of the people, all these ordinances mere shadows looking forward to the perfect sacrifice to come.

For at the right time, Christ would come to fulfill the law and the prophets and to offer his life. God's own Son would be the sacrifice for sins that the blood of animals could never satisfy. As God had promised from the beginning, "the heel" of his Redeemer would be wounded.

Under Moses, the people of Israel wandered in the

desert for forty years. Then Joshua led them into the Promised Land where they conquered Canaan's inhabitants, nations ripe for judgment.

Gradually, the land was settled and each of the twelve tribes received its allotted portion. Of these twelve, Jacob had prophesied that God's promised one would come through the tribe of Judah.

After Joshua's death, "judges" ruled the people during times of trial. But dissatisfied, the people clamored for a king to be like the other nations. This kingship was first established with King Saul perhaps a thousand years before Christ.

Upon Saul's failure, the royal line was established by God's decree with the greatest of Israel's kings, David, born in Bethlehem, of the tribe of Judah. Through David's royal line, "Messiah" would come, who would be none other than the Redeemer promised to Adam and Eve at the fall.

In the long centuries that followed, King Solomon built the great first Temple in Jerusalem; the kingdom divided in two; prophets spoke and wrote; other kings lived and died; the kingdoms each went into captivity and the first Temple was destroyed; but the Jews returned to Judea again by God's promise and rebuilt the Temple.

Then for four hundred years heaven was silent—no prophet spoke in Israel. During that time, the lowly land of Judea was conquered first by the Greeks, and then by the mighty Romans. Where was God? Where was Messiah?

IN THE FULLNESS OF TIME

In the beginning, the Creator of heaven and earth declared to Satan that one born of woman would come to "crush" his head. This son of a woman would do victorious battle with the devil and be a savior to those in helpless bondage to Satan, sin and death.

Yet Adam and Eve died before the fulfillment of God's promise. The flood came, and Noah's family were left to replenish the earth. Generations later, God called Abraham and promised that through his line would come one to be a blessing to all the peoples of the earth. Through Abraham's descendants, God continued to promise with ever greater clarity in divers ways through divers prophets and priests and kings the coming of this one.

By inspired revelation, these prophets and seers proclaimed that this one would be sinless, born of a virgin, born in Bethlehem, of the tribe of Judah, of the lineage of David, called the Prophet, a Priest, a King, a Nazarene, that the government would rest upon his shoulder, he'd come riding on the colt of a donkey, he'd be a shepherd of his people, a light to the Gentiles, a sacrifice for sin, sold for thirty pieces of silver, his body pierced, no bone to be broken, buried in a rich man's tomb, and raised from death on the third day, to name but a few recorded over centuries.

Yet how quietly this promised Redeemer came into the world! Not as a powerful king at the head of an entourage of angels and armies. The infinite Son of God, who had existed for all eternity in perfect happiness with his Father, left heaven for our dark earth to be born of a virgin teenager, a poor young Jewish girl betrothed to a carpenter, who was the supposed father of Jesus the Christ.

Growing up with his family in almost total obscurity, Jesus lived a perfect, sinless life, the first and only one ever in the long history of the human race. He alone of the Jews earned *the blessing* that God promised in his covenant at Mount Sinai for perfect obedience to the law.

Baptized by John in the Jordan, Jesus began his public ministry at age thirty. For three years he traveled throughout Galilee, Samaria and Judea, preaching the good news of God's Kingdom, teaching, healing and working miracles—demonstrating his divinity and anointing to the crowds that followed.

Was Jesus really the long-promised Redeemer? Had Messiah come at last? Even his own disciples wondered and doubted. But Jesus knew who he was (Matt. 11:1-10). He set his face "like a flint" for Jerusalem to fulfill a destiny determined by God before the creation of the world. The Lamb of God had come into the world to take upon himself the sins of mankind, to be the perfect ransom and sacrifice promised at the fall.

In Jerusalem, Jesus confronted the religious elites over their hypocrisy. They planned to kill him. Betrayed by Judas in the Garden of Gethsemane, he was tried on false charges and found guilty. Under pressure, Pilate the

Roman governor had Jesus beaten and then executed by crucifixion.

In the great hatred and animosity poured out upon Jesus in his death, Satan appeared to work his will with impunity. Yet, even as he had promised, God worked his greater will, accomplishing mighty purposes in the death and resurrection of his Son.

Crucified between two common thieves, the innocent Son of God died cruelly at the hands of creatures of his own making. Before he died, he prayed "Father, forgive them, for they do not know what they do" (Lk. 23:34).

But as was promised in the Garden, Satan only wounded "his heel." It was impossible for death to hold the Son of God.

On the third day, Jesus arose victorious. His disciples saw him, and at one point over 500 witnesses saw him, too. After forty days, Jesus ascended before his followers' very eyes to the Father's right hand. There he is seated in glory and honor until he returns again, coming on the clouds of heaven with great majesty and power to judge the living and the dead.

God had made his gracious promise in the presence of Adam and Eve thousands of years before. Yet, God had kept his word! In the fullness of time, the "seed" of the woman had truly come and he had vanquished Satan, sin and death.

God had further promised Abraham that all the families of earth would be blessed through his descendent.

And it came true. The Good News of Christ, the sinless seed of Abraham, is preached to all nations. Believers are baptized in the name of the Father, Son and Holy Spirit and their sins forgiven, opening the way to heaven.

Through the faithful fulfillment of God's ancient promise to send a Savior into the world, countless sons and daughters of Adam and Eve now receive eternal life. By faith in Jesus Christ, they have overcome their dreadful bondage to the three great evil powers arrayed against them.

2

WHY DID HE DIE:
OUR PROPITIATION

"And He Himself is the propitiation for our sins…"
1 John 2:2

WHEN I WAS A BOY, I remember our pastor would read the Ten Commandments aloud from the old Prayer Book once a month. Hearing the list, I knew I was guilty of breaking these commandments in various ways.

But the short response following each commandment asked God to have mercy on us. I understood from these words that God knew I broke his laws along with all the people in the church, yet somehow he was merciful in nature to forgive me when I acknowledged my wrongs and genuinely sought to change.

Then the Priest would read "the comfortable words." He ended with this statement from Saint John: "If any man sin, we have an advocate with the Father, Jesus Christ the righteous: and he is the *propitiation* for our sins" (1 Jn. 2:1b-2a). Though I didn't really know what this word meant, I believed that God somehow graciously accepted me and would help me become a better person.

What I heard in church as a boy shaped my whole concept of God as one who understood my weaknesses and forgave them. I believed in his mercy and grace toward me, as if that's all there was for me to know and understand. I saw only part of God's nature.

What I didn't understand was the extent of God's infinite holy anger toward sin. Because of my lack of understanding, I had no concept of the necessity and purpose for the death of his Son at the cross. I never grasped the full measure of God's righteous anger against sin that was directed at Jesus when he became "the propitiation for our sins."

———◦◦◦———

Summed up in a rare term called "*Propitiation*" is a second great purpose of God in his Son's passion. Both the Apostle John and the Apostle Paul used this term in explaining one of the great teachings of the Christian faith. The doctrine of *Propitiation* is a truth largely ignored or denied today, but true nonetheless, about what Jesus accomplished by his death for us on the cross.

THE GOODNESS OF GOD

The concept of propitiation begins with the goodness of God. That God is good is a truth many people take for granted in America as a result of our nation's biblical heritage. Throughout history, however, this belief has not always been held. Reflecting their fallen makers, the pagan gods were portrayed as dangerous beings with arbitrary, capricious natures and erratic behavior.

But the Bible is unique in the world's spiritual literature for its portrayal of God. This book alone presents a deity of *absolute* goodness and *infinite* righteousness. God's perfect goodness is revealed to us in Holy Scripture as an essential attribute and character of his nature. In him there is *no* darkness or evil *at all.* Unless we understand this truth, the Bible makes no sense.

However, the Biblical concept of goodness means something far different than our current conception of a passive, weak, harmless niceness. The goodness of God is anything but a sweet, weak niceness.

God's goodness burns as a consuming fire of righteousness at war with evil in every form. He cannot tolerate or excuse evil. He is actively and utterly opposed to it. He fights evil; conquers evil; consumes, judges and punishes evil.

The Bible calls this goodness "holiness." God's holiness is so great that the angels in heaven cry day and night in constant praise of his majestic being, "Holy, holy, holy, is the Lord" (Is. 6:3). Fallen creatures that we are, we cannot comprehend such goodness without his grace to help us.

Because God is absolutely good, he zealously demands perfect justice in all his dealings with evil and wickedness. His justice is performed with infinite, righteous, burning anger and indignation towards evil. As fallen sinners, we rightfully fear this terrible burning wrath of God. It terrifies us. We tremble at such goodness, justice and holy anger. We resent it and want to hide from it.

Were God only holy, we would be without any hope

whatsoever. Were he only holy, the human race would have ceased to exist at the fall. But God has been merciful, patient and long-suffering with our sinful race. That we continue to exist is a constant, daily demonstration of his character.

And here, then, is where the concept of propitiation comes in. Because God is good, he *must* judge and punish the evil of guilty sinners. His holy wrath and righteous anger demand it. But the quality of his goodness also calls forth mercy and compassion to forgive the sinful weakness of his creatures. How then does God appease his just and infinite anger and yet provide for our forgiveness? He does so by means of "propitiation."

To propitiate is to appease the anger of another by means of an atoning sacrifice or offering. Propitiation makes it possible for God's holy anger and justice to be satisfied and appeased.

In the case of our sinfulness, this propitiation was neither cheap nor easy. Nor could we provide for our own means of propitiating the anger of God. To appease Almighty God for our evil and restore us to his good favor required nothing less than the death of his own sinless Son.

HUMAN GUILT
The concept of propitiation in the Bible recognizes and deals with the genuine guiltiness of human beings before a holy God. Denying our guiltiness prevents us from being forgiven. Dismissing our guiltiness underestimates

the danger we are in before God's wrath. Denial and dismissal both leave us guilty before him.

As the Bible teaches, human guilt began in the Garden. Our original ancestors fell into sin of their own free will and introduced sin into the human race through natural inheritance. Adam and Eve passed their deformity to their descendents created in their image. As a result, all human beings of every race and every nation and every time come into the world inheriting a nature that is spiritually dead to God with an inborn propensity to sin.

Satan further manipulates this natural human propensity of rebellion and denial before God. Knowingly and unknowingly, humans do Satan's will rather than God's (Eph. 2:1-3). This behavior results in real guilt, not the false guilt that mental health workers so often encounter. Humans seek to hide this real guilt from God who of course knows everything.

It's in part for this reason that God provided the Ten Commandments. He did so not that fallen humans would be able to obey them perfectly—they can't. But his Law is a standard to reveal our guilt as a necessary step towards forgiveness and salvation. If we seek to deceive ourselves about our guilt, the light of God's perfect Law teaches us otherwise. Indeed, James teaches that by breaking even one of God's laws, we stand accused before him of breaking them all (Jam. 2:10)!

As a healthy spiritual practice, the old Episcopal Prayer Book included the famous Confession where we acknowledged before God "our manifold sins and wickedness, which we from time to time, most grievously have committed, by thought, word and deed." It was much as the alcoholic who confessed his alcoholism as the first step to recovery, painful as the truth was. The path to genuine freedom and forgiveness started with owning up to what we are and what we've done.

Of course, we hate the thought of being guilty! But acknowledging our sinfulness and guilt before God prepares us for the biblical solution which is propitiation through the passion of his Son.

BY THE SHEDDING OF BLOOD

Propitiation is the means by which God's *just* wrath against sin's evil is satisfied through a sacrifice. But not just any sacrifice will do. The Bible teaches that without the shedding of blood it's impossible to forgive sin. Since the penalty for sin was death, and "life is in the blood," the Law required the shedding of blood (Lev. 17:14). The legal penalty of death was exacted with the shedding of blood (Heb. 9:22).

Because the entire human race is guilty before God, therefore each and every person deserves eternal death and punishment for sin. So when God in mercy determined to provide a means to propitiate his anger toward human sinners, his just wrath still required the shedding of blood. There had to be a sacrifice of death.

However, this sacrifice should not be confused with the pagan, barbarian concept of bribing a blood-thirsty deity, as if the almighty God needs anything from us that he could not provide himself. All that exists does so by God's own creation. He needs nothing from his creatures.

Rather the sacrifice God required was to serve the purpose of holy justice. The sacrifice that would appease his anger must be the fair, just and sufficient provision commensurate with the crime. The shedding of blood for sin was a matter of justice and fairness.

This concept of sacrifice was understood by the Jews. The Law of Moses established the practice of animal sacrifice for the covering for sins. Every year the High Priest offered the sacrifice of blood from innocent, unblemished animals upon the altar of God. This practice was performed in the original Tabernacle in the wilderness and later in the first, second and third temples.

God introduced this practice to teach his chosen people the lesson that without the shedding of blood there could be no forgiveness. Forgiveness was never just a matter of simply overlooking offenses or dismissing the seriousness of sin. True justice demanded otherwise. By the shedding of blood, justice could be served. However, instead of the sinner's death, God's wrath could be appeased by the sacrifice of a substitutionary death.

Yet because the blood of bulls and goats could not truly take away human sin, each year the Jews had to continually repeat their sacrifices and offerings. Human sin required the shedding of human blood. The sacrifice of animals only pointed to the ultimate sacrifice that God himself would provide, as he'd promised in the Garden.

WITH HIS OWN BLOOD

If human blood must be shed for human sin, how could any human blood ever atone for sin since "all have sinned and fall short of the glory of God"? (Rom. 3:23). No natural descendent of Adam could ever hope to offer a sufficient sacrifice. All humans needed atonement for sin.

The solution to this dilemma could only come from God himself, for whom nothing is impossible. God would provide the perfect sacrifice to satisfy his own justice and wrath against sin. He would do so through the sacrifice of his only Son. His son would come into the world to save sinners by means of his passion and death. Though guiltless, he would be unfairly tried through a court of law and executed as an act of "legal justice."

Christ came for this very purpose, determined by God before humans were even created. Jesus was not a helpless victim, but the obedient Son of his Father come to fulfill the plan of God even unto death.

Born without a sinful nature through the miracle of the virgin birth, Jesus was perfect God and perfect man. Though tempted as we are, he lived a sinless life. "Can any of you accuse me of sin?" he asked (Jn. 8:46a).

A sinless human being, Jesus Christ alone could offer his life as a sufficient sacrifice to God for sin. By the shedding of his own blood—a life of infinite value as the Son of God—he could provide the necessary sacrifice to appease or propitiate God's wrath. In the agony of his death and in his unjust execution at the hands of sinners, he provided once for all the propitiation for sin.

Because Jesus was both God and man, the sacrifice of his one perfect life accomplished what no animal sacrifice could ever do. He was the "Lamb of God" slain in his Father's foreknowledge and plan before any human sinned (Jn. 1:29, 36).

On the cross, Jesus' blood was poured out before his Father for the sins of the whole world: for through him all the families of the earth would be blessed, not just Jews but Gentiles, too. The death of his infinite, almighty Son was God's amazing propitiation offered to a race of fallen sinners in rebellion to his holy rule.

FAITH IN HIS BLOOD

For Christ's propitiation to take effect in a person's life, God has ordained that it be received "by faith" (Rom. 3:22-28, 30). Individuals must acknowledge their guilt for sin and believe that God has provided a sacrifice for this sin, not just in some general sense, but in the specific sense that Christ satisfied God's wrath for *their* sin by shedding his blood on the cross.

No superstitious faith that Christ's blood has "magical" potency, true faith simply believes that the offering of his life through the shedding of his blood was sufficient to pay for sin. In this way, faith transfers the work of Christ on the cross to the life of the individual believer.

This faith at once believes God's testimony in his own word that his promise is true and the work done. This faith trusts in the character of God to do such a thing and to have kept his promise to do so to his great glory.

God's moral goodness and justice is also seen in the fact that the benefits of this propitiation are not simply applied to everyone "across the board" in a meaningless fashion. For the sacrifice to be appropriated a measure of moral response is required on the part of a human being: *faith*, which itself is a gift of God (Eph. 2:8).

This faith depends upon God to do what the sinner could never do. God is therefore glorified for his goodness and mercy in providing propitiation at such cost to himself for helpless sinners.

Far from a crude, barbaric appeasement of a vengeful, bloodthirsty god, Christ's propitiation is a high and holy concept flowing from God's absolute goodness, righteousness and holiness. The sacrifice of his own Son demonstrates the magnitude of his incomprehensible compassion and love for lost sinners on one hand and his fearful and absolute righteousness on the other.

In this way, Jesus Christ delivered us from the penalty of eternal punishment and death, having satisfied the requirement of God's perfect law and justice by means of his propitiation. For our iniquities he was bruised—a propitiation to God that is ours by faith.

3

WHY DID HE DIE:
OUR REDEMPTION

"...through the redemption that is in Christ Jesus."
Romans 3:24b

WHEN I BEGAN seriously reading God's Word for the first time at age twenty-six, I was enormously ignorant about my previous spiritual bondage to powers greater than myself.

While I had known as a boy that I committed sins, I didn't know why. I even knew that I seemed at times to be utterly helpless to stop doing things I knew to be wrong. Then I would become overcome with guilt and remorse, only to have this same scenario happen all over again the next time I did something wrong. I knew nothing about the *principle* of sin at work in my nature.

As for believing in the reality of the devil, to me that belief was mere superstition. I had never given any real consideration to the thought of him. To my mind, the devil was only a figment of the imagination, a folk carry-over from the Middle Ages, a convenient subject for jokes.

Death, however, was a reality to me. First I feared it for members of my family. Eventually, I feared dying myself without accomplishing anything.

But I had no understanding of the idea of spiritual

death as separation from God. Nor had I ever thought about the afterlife. I'm not sure I completely doubted the concept of heaven; to me heaven was basically irrelevant. I was living in this life. All my dreams and desires were here. Nor had I any fear of judgment.

Without the scriptures, I could never have known the true extent of my spiritual condition. As I discovered, like all human beings, I'd been born in bondage to three terrible powers. To be free, I needed a Redeemer to pay the ransom for my release.

———— ◆◇◆ ————

A third great purpose of God in the passion of his Son is one the Bible calls *"redemption."* Christ our Redeemer purchased a people back for God from Satan, sin and death. His life was the ransom paid to redeem us from bondage to these evil powers.

Sold in sin

In their fall, Adam and Eve sold themselves and all their future progeny in a terrible transaction with evil. Not only did they enslave themselves to evil masters, but of such great consequence to the whole human race, along with themselves they sold *all their descendents that would be born through them*, too.

Just as children born to slaves automatically become slaves, so here. By law, the children of slaves become the property of their master. In our case, Satan, sin and death became masters of the whole human race, a right they gained through the disobedience of our first ancestors.

Because the Bible teaches that all human beings ultimately trace their ancestry back through Noah to Adam, all humans were affected by Adam's tragic fall. Through the fall, every individual descendent of every family of every race and language and nation on earth was brought into bondage by inherited nature (Gal. 3:22).

Save for Jesus, in all the world's long history, no baby, no child, no man, no woman has ever been exempted from this sad inheritance. As the Bible teaches, "the wicked are estranged from the womb; they go astray as soon as they are born, speaking lies" (Ps. 58:3), and "There is none righteous, no, not one" (Rom. 3:10b).

Of course, any honest person knows the consequence of the fall to be true by simple observation. We acknowledge that no human being is exempt from a propensity to do evil. Our fallen natures are a fact of human existence. No amount of wishful thinking or denial can escape this fact.

And because all human beings are born into this bondage, if they are ever to be free, all are equally in need of *redemption*.

This concept of redemption was well-established in the ancient world. An economic value was placed upon a slave for the remaining duration of his or her useful life. By paying this sum, a slave could even purchase back his own freedom. The Jews also recognized the practice of the "kinsman redeemer" as a pattern for the great redemption to come. A family member could restore property to another family member by means of paying a price.

But what would be the price for the eternal redemption of the highest order of God's creation on earth—human beings made in his image? Redeeming us from our lost state would require something of equal or greater value. What could provide for such a costly redemption? What could be of such incalculable value? What could suffice to redeem a multitude of sinners from their bondage to Satan, sin and death?

Surely not silver and gold. Surely not the blood of bulls and goats. Nothing less than the infinitely valuable sinless life of the Son of God in human form could pay the price of our redemption.

So Christ came to join the long continuity of the human race that he might set us free. Christ, the sinless "last Adam," came at the cost of his life to redeem the sons and daughters of the first Adam from their bondage to three evil masters (Rom. 3:22-23; 1 Cor. 15:45).

REDEEMED FROM SATAN

By submitting to the serpent's deception, Adam and Eve brought themselves under Satan's sway and dominion. In their ignorance they became Satan's slaves for the purpose of evil. They chose to do *his* will of their own *free* will.

By choosing evil, they chose to replace God as their master. In God's place, the devil became their master. And through Adam and Eve, Satan gained a permanent right and power over the human race descended from them.

As the Bible reveals, the devil is "the spirit who now works in the sons of disobedience" (Eph. 2:2b) and he is "the wicked one" under whose sway the whole world now lies (1 Jn. 5:18b). The condition of humanity is not quite like the story of Daniel Webster and the devil, where Daniel sells his soul to the devil. In our case, the devil already has the human race in his grasp. All human beings are born into this bondage and must be redeemed if they're ever to escape.

Nor is it that humans could escape of their own accord if they only knew about their bondage to this invisible master of deceit and intimidation. First, even if denial were not the normal human response to this truth, no human by sheer will-power alone could ever escape the devil's sway. Satan's power is so great that no human being could every hope to overpower him and flee.

Secondly, even if human beings could escape, by their fallen nature humans are the devil's willing subjects and gladly do his will, even if unknowingly. The earth is not more wicked than it is only because of God's wise providence. He provides external checks to limit human behavior: through man-made laws, rewards, status, what people might think, etc., and death itself.

For this reason, the appearance of good behavior often has more to do with deeper motives of self-interest than any principle of goodness for the glory of God. And in this way Satan is still at work in the sons of disobedience.

What therefore can be done? How can any human escape the bondage of a being so powerful?

The good news of the gospel is that Jesus Christ came into the world to save sinners and "to be a ransom for many." In this glorious endeavor, the devil could not resist him. The devil tried his best, but merely "bruised his heel." He could not overpower Christ. When Jesus died on the cross, his priceless death was a ransom to repurchase us for God.

At the cross, the Son of God defeated the power of the devil and freed believers from satanic bondage. By his passion, Jesus Christ redeemed all those who would receive his death by faith as a full and just compensation for their sin.

The death and resurrection of Jesus proved to be the mortal blow God first promised in the Garden to "crush the head" of the evil one and his evil interests. As we learn in the New Testament, it's now but a matter of time before Satan is destroyed eternally in the Lake of Fire.

REDEEMED FROM SIN

As slaves of sin, humans could never hope to free themselves from its oppressive yoke on their own, either. How could such a thing be possible? By definition, everything slaves do and everything they own is already not theirs to begin with. What then could humans ever offer or produce to redeem themselves from their awful master sin?

The power of sin totally controlled human personality. If we doubt this truth, consider Jesus' words, "anyone who sins is a slave of sin" (Jn. 8:34b). The Book of Romans further teaches it's impossible for the fallen human nature to *ever* obey God for purely right principles (Rom. 8:7).

Sin in the human nature always corrupts everything that every human being has ever done apart from the grace and work of God in a human life. Such is the power of sin in the human heart.

Christ, however, as perfect God and perfect man was without sin. Therefore he could offer his life as a sufficient sacrifice to pay for sin and our redemption. As God's Son, his life was of infinite value and worth. No debt for sin could be so great that his life and death were not enough—no amount of human sin could be so great as to count his infinite life insufficient for the price.

In a miraculous supernatural transaction, Christ absorbed the sin of the world, becoming sin for us. At that moment God's judgment fell entirely upon his own Son. He paid the price in full.

By dying for sin, Christ acted like the Old Testament kinsman redeemer who by law could buy back the property of his relatives. On the cross, Christ died for sin to buy us back from bondage.

Finite sin, as great in total as it's been in the world's long, cruel, dark history, was no match for the value of the priceless, perfect, infinite life of Jesus freely offered to redeem the lost from sin.

REDEEMED FROM DEATH

Christ redeemed his people not only from the dark powers of sin and Satan, but also from a third power death.

Tyrant death entered the human race through the fall of Adam and Eve. From that occasion on, death ruled over all humanity. As the Bible tells us, and we know by sad experience, death is appointed once to every person (Heb. 9:27).

Humans however were not created to die. We were created to live forever. The Tree of Life was originally planted in the Garden for this reason. Our first ancestors and their descendants were to eat from this tree and live without ever dying. But Adam and Eve had a choice and chose death.

Of course God knew the outcome of their probation before Adam and Eve were created. Rather, from the foundation of the earth, he planned to send a Redeemer as he promised who would suffer the penalty of death for us.

At the perfect time, this redeemer Christ came into the world. And though he did not deserve death, and was unjustly sentenced to death for no crime of his own, God's will was that Christ suffer death, and thereby defeat death by overcoming it.

In this way, God did not simply annul death and make it go away. How could he? Death was his own righteous decree for sin. But by experiencing death on our behalf, Christ was able to offer his death as a ransom for ours. Because the Son of God was greater than death, death could not hold him. He rose again from the dead.

Now all who believe in Christ and his work on the cross receive his death on their behalf—his blood shed for them—that they in turn might live forever, freed from bondage to death and the fear of death that's held the human race in bondage from the beginning.

I KNOW THAT MY REDEEMER LIVES

In what may be the Bible's oldest book, Job proclaimed an enduring faith in the promise of a personal redeemer and the resurrection of the body after death. In his darkest moments, Job declared he would see his redeemer "stand at the latter day upon the earth" (Job 19:25).

In so doing, Job testified to his belief in God's ancient promise. He also revealed his faith in the bodily resurrection. How else could Job hope to see his redeemer stand physically upon the earth long after Job himself had died—unless he too were to be raised physically from death.

In his own simple words, Job had reaffirmed the biblical doctrine of redemption. He was assured that one would come to redeem him from the powers of darkness and death. Job looked forward to the coming of the one who would be Jesus Christ.

It was Christ who would come to fulfill the promise of God. In so doing, he would propitiate God's wrath for sin and redeem believers from the three-fold power of Satan, sin and death. In giving his life as a ransom for many, Christ would purchase us back for God, offering his perfect, sinless life to redeem our sinful, broken lives.

Who can conceive of the value of the life of the infinite Son of God who created the universe? Yet by giving up his life for ours, he conferred great value on us and our eternal souls. The intrinsic value of our lives is as the dust of the earth. But redeemed by the infinitely valuable life of Christ, our lives become of incalculable value to God and to ourselves.

Without faith, it's impossible to appropriate to ourselves the redemption purchased at such great cost by God's Son. Like Job, we must apply this doctrine of redemption to our lives by faith. This faith in Christ's passion makes our redemption from bondage possible.

4

WHY DID HE DIE:
OUR JUSTIFICATION

"...justified freely by his grace..." Romans 3:24

IN MY FIRST YEAR back in church, a well-known African bishop preached one Sunday morning. During his message I let out an uncontrollable sob. My cry was so loud that our minister came to me after the service and asked if I was all right.

A wave of grief and relief had washed over me. How was it possible that God could really forgive me for all I had done? I had wandered so far away from what I had intended in my life and had once known to be right. How could I ever forgive myself?

I regretted hurting so many people. I'd lied, broken my word, stolen property, taken drugs, dishonored my parents, lived immorally, committed adultery, pressed for the abortion of my own baby, and outspokenly rejected God in every way. If it were not for the life I'd led and the selfish decisions I'd made, I could have done so much good instead.

It took me several years to resolve some of these issues, before the full conviction settled in my mind and heart that God had truly forgiven me. Some of this slow process was due to inconsistent teachings that I heard. Some was due to the time I needed to learn and heal.

God had his own purpose and was in no hurry.

But in due time I came to grasp the true extent to which Christ had borne my guilt through his death and that in turn his perfect righteousness was imputed to me by faith. In true legal terms I had been found to be "justified" in God's eyes and acquitted. I was no longer guilty before him.

———◆◆◆———

The Bible declares Almighty God to be the Judge of the living and the dead. Our eternal Judge existed before all time, through all generations, and will continue after time ceases to be. This infinite, eternal Being will judge all humans in the strictest accounting of sin imaginable: no thought, word or action will escape his notice and holy judgment (Heb. 4:12-13).

What hope have fallen human beings before such a Judge? He cannot deny our sin or pretend it doesn't exist, and, as God, he's bound by his own nature to punish sin and hold us accountable.

For this reason, the Bible's teaching on justification is so essential to our faith. Our justification before the Judge of all the earth-whereby God makes sinners justified and guiltless in his sight-is a fourth great purpose in the passion of Christ.

EVERYONE IS GUILTY

The retort: "No one is perfect!" is a frequent response to human failure. Everyone knows it to be true. But why do we know it's true? The reason is any honest observer of the human condition understands that people—all people—at one time or other think bad thoughts, say bad words, do bad deeds, and fail to do or not to do what they ought to do.

In fact, this type of behavior is so common that we all tend to justify our lives by relative standards, rather than absolute ones. We think we're doing a pretty good job because we believe we're somewhat better than the next person. Or we think we're not as bad as we could be. Or we truly make an effort to behave rightly most of the time.

However, when judged by absolute standards, we're all found wanting. The whole world stands guilty before God!

Jesus, the only sinless man to ever walk the earth, saw our race in such absolute terms. God's infallible Son referred to his hearers as, "If you then, being evil..." (Matt. 7:19). In declaring them evil, he gave the divine perspective. Heaven's assessment of human nature was now utterly changed from original God's declaration at creation which was "very good."

This passage is not an isolated one. The Bible also tells us that after the fall God "saw that the wickedness of man was great in the earth, and that every imagination of the thoughts of his heart was only evil continually" (Gen. 6:5). Here we see a litany of absolutes referring to human depravity and evil. Thousands of years later, the prophet Jeremiah could write, "the heart is deceitful above all things, and desperately wicked, who can know it?" (Jer. 17:9).

Naturally, we don't like to think of ourselves in these terms. We want to think these descriptions applied to people then, but we've improved now by education and evolution. But the Bible is realistic. Scripture tells us the truth about human nature from God's holy perspective. In it, we see our nature contrasted with his absolute perfection and goodness.

Again, the great purpose of the Ten Commandments was to expose human fault and sinfulness in absolute terms. But God had a higher reason for doing so. His perfect Law is like a school teacher. As it teaches us our guilt, we learn we need a savior (Gal. 3:23-24).

In this way, God's holy Law is actually a merciful thing. Like a doctor, it tells us the honest truth about our condition, so we take necessary action. Denial leads only to eternal death.

But seeing our true condition in light of God's holy standards can lead us to salvation. The Law warns of the futility of any false dependence upon our own righteousness. It points us to a true dependence upon God's mercy and grace to forgive sinners through faith in Jesus Christ.

GOD IS THE JUDGE

Over and over again, scripture reveals God to be the supreme Judge of the world: "And the heavens proclaim his righteousness, for God himself is judge" (Ps. 50:6).

The glorious heaven is his courtroom. There he presides as the sole judge and jury before whom we're accountable. He will judge the living and the dead.

Now this perfect, infinite, almighty, eternal Being who is to be our Judge sees all and knows all. He's also just, impartial, and a consuming fire of righteousness and goodness, absolutely opposed to evil in any form, small or great. To break one of his laws is to be guilty of breaking them all.

Every thought, every word, every deed of every life in every age has been exposed to his holy gaze. There is no time in history, no place on earth hidden from his penetrating sight. His standard is absolute perfection. There can be and will be no excuses.

If we tremble before human magistrates and government power in the hands of mere mortals, how much more should we tremble before this omnipotent Being if we dare to stand upon our own righteousness. We fool ourselves to think he'll wink at our misdeeds, or that the petty righteousness of even the best humans could ever bear his blazing justice.

In the face of such implacable justice, there could be only despair without a Savior. No denial could save us. No luck could deliver us. No karma would be sufficient. We'd be without hope.

As the Bible reveals there will be a Judgment Day before the great Judge in heaven. Scripture teaches that it's appointed once for every one to die, and then comes judgment (Heb. 9:27).

Thankfully, in this terrible court of Law, our deliverance lies not in our selves but in the one who came for our *justification*.

CHRIST IS OUR ADVOCATE

God's Word tells us that besides our great Judge in the court of heaven, there will also be an Advocate (Jn. 2:1). He is Jesus Christ the righteous. Jesus died and rose again for our justification and appears in heaven on behalf of all who trust in him.

But the devil would present us with two temptations to turn our attention from Christ. One is to believe that our sins are so great we could never be forgiven by God, and our situation is hopeless. We could never meet God's holy standards, so all is lost.

The other temptation is exactly the opposite: to think we're not so bad after all compared to others, or that God's standards could never be so strict. Surely our good deeds outweigh our bad, and no loving God would ever hold us accountable in any way that could be truly serious.

In both cases the devil is a liar and a deceiver.

Clearly, God is not opposed in principle to anyone earning their way to heaven, if such a thing were humanly possible. After all, Jesus lived a sinless life, and he earned *the blessing* promised to Moses under the old covenant. But except for Jesus, no one else, corrupted as we are by sin, has ever kept or ever can keep God's Law perfectly.

Therefore God would not have us deceived into false security by a sense of our own supposed goodness. God is not about to lower the bar of his standards. Though we might want it so, lowering God's standards is not the answer to salvation.

Yet, because God's bar is set so high doesn't mean sinners are without hope. Christ died, the righteous for the unrighteous. His death was God's perfect sacrifice and offering for our sins and the sins of the whole world. God did not lower his standards, nor did he deny our sin. Rather, at the greatest cost, he paid the full price for our justification himself—the death of his beloved Son.

And it's his own Son, the resurrected Christ, who is our Advocate in heaven's holy court. Christ is not there to argue our goodness or to discount the gravity of our sin. Christ is there to argue the sufficiency of his death in our place. He is arguing that on the cross, he legally became sin for us—bearing the sins of the world in his own body—and that being cursed in our place, he made a full, perfect and complete satisfaction for God's justice and the Law's requirements.

BEING JUSTIFIED BY FAITH

Appearing on our behalf, could Christ our Advocate ever lose his case for our justification before heaven's court? Impossible!

The Bible teaches that "while we were yet sinners" and at "enmity with God," the Father sent his only Son into the world to save us (Rom. 5:5, 8:7). God appointed

Christ to this very task. His mission was according to God's own promise!

Furthermore, Christ's perfect obedience to God on earth fulfilled the Law's requirements. The offering of his sinless life paid our debt of eternal death for sin. His resurrection demonstrated that he had made full satisfaction for the Law's demands.

Having ascended to heaven in his resurrected body, Christ now appears in the court of God for the vindication and justification of all believers. Proving his case before the great Judge, Christ assures their justification in God's holy court of law.

Therefore, whatever the devil would whisper otherwise in our hearts is a lie. Whatever our emotions would say to us is of no real consequence. God has promised that he justifies all who put their faith in Christ.

This justification before our Maker and Judge is a new legal standing. It's a finding of "not guilty" by heaven's court.

Christ was found guilty for us. He was bruised for our iniquities. He paid the penalty on our behalf. He died in our place.

Free from God's wrath, there is no more threat of punishment for us. God, the Justifier of the unrighteous, justified us through Christ. By justifying us, he remits our sins, takes them away and forgives us fully: past, present and future.

No longer guilty before God, we're restored to a righteous standing before the Judge of heaven and earth.

There is now no condemnation.

Indeed, by faith, Christ's very righteousness is imputed to us just as it was to Abraham when he was justified by faith. As the scripture says, "Abraham believed God, and it was counted to him as righteousness;" and again, "However, to the man who does not work but trusts God who justifies the wicked, his faith is credited as righteousness" (Rom. 4:3, 5).

THE JUST SHALL LIVE BY FAITH

Faith therefore is the means by which we appropriate this justification to ourselves. When we believe God's promises in his Word, we demonstrate our trust in Him and his good intentions toward us in Christ.

To doubt, deny or reject God's promises is to call God a liar. We remain in our sin and unbelief, a state of spiritual death.

But when we believe in Christ, his work is applied to us. We're considered "just" because he is just. We live in him by faith. As scripture teaches, it's not by works of the law on our part that we're saved, but by faith in Christ's work (Gal. 2:16).

This faith means much more than mere intellectual acceptance of the information. It calls for true dependence upon the death and resurrection of Jesus Christ for our own personal justification. His death really paid for *our* sin. His rising again from death proved his total victory over *our* sin.

If Christ had never died, we'd still be in our sins. If

Christ had not risen again, we could never trust that he was victorious. We could never be assured that his life and death were sufficient for our salvation. What hope could we have then of deliverance from sin's dread penalty of death?

Without Christ's death and resurrection, God's promise in the Garden would remain unfulfilled. Yet these events did take place in history, even as God promised they would in the beginning.

By faith in the death and resurrection of Jesus Christ, we understand that we've been truly forgiven and we will be resurrected to everlasting life and have escaped eternal punishment. By faith in his death and resurrection for us, we can know with certainty that we've been justified before Almighty God, the Judge of heaven and earth.

5

WHY DID HE DIE:
OUR RECONCILIATION

"...we were reconciled to him through the death of his Son..."
Romans 5:10b

DURING THE YEARS that I had become a professing atheist, I believed the idea of "God" was a crutch for weak
people who couldn't face the emptiness of life and the
fears of existence on their own. Just like the Israelites
of old, I'd forgotten my earlier experience of God's presence and reality.

My first real doubts began during my junior year in
college. My fiancée's father died suddenly of cancer as a
relatively young man. I was not bitter, but I prayed every
night for him to live, and yet he died. It seemed unfair to
me and made no sense. I began to think perhaps there
really was no God. Because of my lifestyle, doubting his
existence became more convenient as well.

At the same time, news reports of the war in Viet-
nam portrayed an ugly struggle that seemed senseless to
me. Stories of chaotic battlefield encounters made life
and death look utterly happenstance and meaningless.

Later, I could see that I'd been looking at these trag-
edies from my own selfish, self-centered perspective.
Reading Paul's Letter to the Romans, I learned that human beings naturally suppress the knowledge of the truth

about God. We know he exists, but to serve our own ends, we deny it.

A sinful fallen creature, I was naturally at enmity with God. I had been at war with him and separated from him by my sin without even knowing it.

Yet God had graciously restored me to fellowship with himself through Jesus Christ. Redeeming me through the death of his own beloved Son and justifying me in his sight, God had made it possible for me to be reconciled to him. I'm now at peace with my Maker.

———◦✸◦———

A fifth great purpose of God in the passion of Christ was to reconcile lost sinners to a right relationship with himself. For God who is holy cannot be in relationship with that which is unholy. God is at war with evil. Yet, in his love, he would reconcile us to himself.

Therefore to accomplish this *reconciliation*, he would sacrifice the life of his only Son.

BROKEN RELATIONSHIP

Most people live their whole lives completely unaware that they're not in a right relationship with God. If they believe in his existence at all, they assume that this holy Being just naturally accepts them as they are, as if it were his duty to do so.

Nothing could be further from the truth.

Before the fall, our first ancestors enjoyed a perfect relationship with the good and holy God in whose image they were created. Their Creator, an infinite, righteous being, condescended to have an intimate fellowship with these two finite creatures of his own making. He held daily communion with them in the Garden.

No sin existed to break the wondrous relationship they enjoyed. This relationship of the first humans with their holy Creator was possible because he had himself declared them to be "good" upon their making, even "very good."

But in their probation, our first parents disobeyed God of their own free will. Believing the serpent that tempted them, they ate of the Tree of the Knowledge of Good and Evil. Before this, they had only known goodness. Evil they had never known.

Suddenly, upon this one act of disobedience, they knew evil first hand. This knowledge was not intellectual only, but experiential. It changed their very natures permanently and corrupted them.

In absolute terms, they had done evil. By one act, they had become no longer good, and could not go back and undo what they had done to be perfectly good again. It was impossible.

Furthermore, evil was absolutely opposed to God. The free and open fellowship they had known with their Creator was now broken beyond human repair.

How could light have fellowship with darkness? As the scriptures teach, "Your iniquities have separated you from your God" (Isa. 59:2a). Sin would cut the human race off from its Maker.

CHILDREN OF WRATH

As a consequence of the fall, the corrupted human race descended into great rebellion against God. Sin was passed on from generation to generation. Fallen, sinful human beings produced fallen, sinful children. No so-called "evolutionary progress" improved human nature.

No amount of education or culture could remove this sin from the human heart, either. At best sin would be channeled in ways less harmful and the grace of God would provide checks against its unlimited expression.

Born in sin and bound by sin, human beings became not children of God, reflecting his image, but children of the devil and children of wrath. Not simply separated from God in some passive way by their sin, sinful humans now fell under God's active wrath—his holy anger and opposition to sin and evil in all its forms.

As Paul's letter to the Ephesians declares of the Gentiles, "you were without hope and without God in the world." We were without God because sin had separated us from him. We were without hope because nothing we could do on our own could change this awful circumstance.

As a consequence, we faced certain eternal damnation without escape on Judgment Day. The holy justice of God required punishment for evil to be dispensed. Only condemnation and everlasting misery and destruction awaited us at the hand of Almighty God.

This is the true and honest picture of the human condition presented by the Bible. Separated from God, we could do nothing to save ourselves or help ourselves.

Yet God in his eternal and infinite forbearance did not destroy us as he had every right to do. He allowed us to live that he might fulfill his promise to our ancestors and extend mercy to our race. With patient love for us, God looked forward to the sacrificial offering of Jesus Christ that he might restore us to a right relationship again.

BUT ONE MEDIATOR

Consider the amazing promise God had made before Adam and Eve. A man would be born of a woman so mighty *he* would defeat the devil, sin and death. Could any power be great enough to destroy these mortal enemies of the human race, but God?

But how could God ever be born of a woman? Why would God do such a thing? Yet, over many centuries with ever greater clarity, the prophets proclaimed this very thing must occur, though even to them it remained a mystery.

Then just as promised, it came to pass. A virgin bore a Son conceived of the Holy Spirit without the aid of a human father. Her child had two natures: fully human by his mother's conception, fully divine by the miraculous working of the Holy Spirit. Jesus Christ, the Son of God, had come to bridge the chasm between the infinite Almighty God and a finite sinful race.

As God's Son, Jesus revealed to men the true nature of the invisible Father. He told his disciples, "If you have seen me, you have seen the Father" (Jn. 14:9). "No one has ever seen God," John wrote. "...but God the only Son, who is at the Father's side, has made him known" (Jn. 1:18).

Similarly, Jesus became fully human. He lived and suffered as we do. Indeed, no temptation overtakes us that Jesus didn't also experience and defeat. Yet tempted in every way as we are, he remained without sin. Then he gave himself to die on the cross for our salvation.

Jesus had come from heaven for this purpose. By paying for sin and appeasing God's wrath at the cross, he could bring the opposing parties together. Delivering us from guilt and judgment, Christ made it possible to restore us to a right relationship with our Creator. Former enemies of God, we could now be made his friends, even his own children (Jn. 15:15; Rom 8:15-17).

Through his life, death and resurrection, Jesus Christ became the only Mediator between God and man. No one else could fulfill his office. No angel from heaven could perform it. No other human could accomplish the task. Everyone else but Christ has sinned. No amount of money, nor any amount of gifts, could suffice to reconcile our differences. Jesus Christ alone could fulfill God's promise and mediate between his Father and the human race to bring us together.

BE RECONCILED TO GOD

Having offered up his own Son, God now calls us therefore to be reconciled to him. Christ has died. Christ has risen. Nothing more is needed but for us to respond to the offer of reconciliation. Paul wrote, "...we implore you on Christ's behalf, be reconciled to God" (2 Cor. 5:20b).

God's gracious act to reconcile us to himself through Christ is received on our part by faith. This faith believes in God's promise and trusts in the sufficiency of Christ's work to reconcile us to God and save us from the wrath to come. This faith is further evidenced by a changed life that turns from sin and pursues God's will in the power of his Spirit.

Forgiven of our sins through Christ, the obstacle that separated us from God is removed. Instead the righteousness of Christ is imputed to us by faith. Our broken relationship with God is restored. We have peace with God where there was war.

Beyond this, God makes us more than mere creatures in his kingdom. He lifts us up with Christ into his very own family. Through Christ, we're adopted into the household of God. By faith, we become his very own children, his own extended family.

Working in our hearts, the Spirit of God confirms this new relationship, as we can cry out to God, "Abba, Father" (Rom. 8:15). No longer is he our Creator only, under whose wrath we lived day to day, God becomes our heavenly Father with whom we have an eternal existence.

As God's children, we become his heirs as well. In a remarkable change of circumstance, God demonstrates the abundance of our reconciliation through Christ. He makes us, who were once his enemies and the objects of his anger, to be the inheritors of all that he has.

This amazing gift of reconciliation with God comes to us through Christ. In God's great eternal purpose, revealed at its proper time, Christ made a way for us to be reconciled to our holy Maker.

THE MINISTRY OF RECONCILIATION

Restoring believers to a right relationship with himself, God also honors us with a place in his work of reconciliation with others. This privilege is for all believers. As Jesus promised, we would be his witnesses through the Holy Spirit's power (Acts 1:8).

As witnesses for Christ, we engage in God's work of reconciliation in three ways.

First, the Holy Spirit breaks the bondage of the human will to the power of sin and we become changed people. He sets us free through Christ to love and serve God and others.

A changed life is a powerful witness to the truth and reality of our supernatural God because truly loving God and others before ourselves is not humanly possible aside from divine intervention. In changing us, he demonstrates his great power and grace.

Second, the Holy Spirit gives us "the mind of Christ" to understand the Gospel and holy boldness to share it. The Gospel's spiritual message is closed to the natural mind, blinded by Satan. But the Holy Spirit helps us comprehend it and gives us grace to overcome our fears (1 Cor. 2:14-16).

Fearful, timid men, the first disciples were changed when the Holy Spirit filled them. Immediately, they began to speak God's truth with boldness and courage (Acts 4:23-31).

Third, the Holy Spirit gives spiritual gifts and works through God's people with supernatural power. His Spirit works in ways small and great: from simple answers to prayer, to ways that defy human ability and logic, such as divine healings, special knowledge, prophecies and more.

For Christians this ministry of reconciliation is not an option. Jesus commanded us to go into all the world and make disciples for his kingdom. We're to share God's truth in appropriate ways in our immediate circumstances—with family, friends, neighbors, coworkers, and others with whom we have contact. We're to pray and support those called to special work in serving others and sharing the Gospel. We're to respond when God calls us to serve him in the greater world.

Without Christ's death, we'd have no such good news to share. We'd be lost ourselves and isolated from God. But in mercy and compassion, God saved us and sends us to be ambassadors to a dying world—that they too might be reconciled to him through faith in Jesus Christ.

6

WHY DID HE DIE:
OUR SANCTIFICATION

"For this is the will of God, even your sanctification"
1 Thessalonians 4:3

WITH MY SECOND STEPFATHER, my pattern had been to
avoid him as much as possible. It wasn't that I disliked
him; it was just that, whenever he saw me, he had to find
something for me to do around the house or in the yard.
Most of the time it seemed to me pointless busy work.
Because of his eccentricities, my brother and I made fun
of him to our friends.

But after I started reading the Bible and sitting under preaching, the Holy Spirit began to change me. One
promise had a particularly profound impact upon me:
"If any man be in Christ, he is a new creation" (2 Cor.
5:17a). This revelation utterly amazed me.

For one, I realized I should honor my stepfather and
show him respect. By then he'd developed an advanced
case of Parkinson's disease and was deteriorating quickly.

Moving back home, I helped my mother care for
him for the next two and a half years. Before I had
laughed at him and avoided him; now I fed him, brushed
his teeth, dressed him, cleaned him and put him to bed
on a daily basis until he died.

During this time, I worked full time for a local

company as a writer. Almost every morning, I was up early to attend Bible Studies and prayer meetings. Involved in visiting people and church activities, I came home late each night. Most days I was so tired I wondered how I could continue. I came home wishing I could just go to bed but had to care for Bill first.

After caring for my stepfather, I'd still go up to kneel by my bed to pray, sometimes falling asleep with my head on the edge, praying for my family, friends, neighbors, our church, and missions around the world.

As a discipline, I'd begun to pray daily for the Chinese, Hindus, Muslims, Buddhists and other peoples who didn't know Christ. I'd been given this privilege and found it hard to go to bed without praying for millions who didn't know him as I did. God had put his love in my heart for people to know him for eternity.

❖◈❖

The word *"sanctification"* comes from the Latin word sanctus, or "holy." A sanctuary is a holy place.

In heaven, we're told, the angels cry day and night in glorious, unending worship of the great triune Being and His wondrous nature: "Holy, holy, holy, is the Lord God."

But we are unholy. And sanctification is the process whereby the unholy is made holy by God.

Here then is a sixth great purpose in the passion of God's Son: our sanctification-that we who believe in him are made holy by him, set apart for the Master's use.

Spiritual Rebirth

Jesus told Nicodemus that unless he was "born again" or "born from above," he could never so much as see the kingdom of God. Jesus was talking about spiritual rebirth.

As a consequence of the fall, all humans are born "dead in trespasses and sins" (Eph. 2:1). This death is a spiritual death. While physically alive and able to eat and breathe and think and talk, we're dead spiritually by nature. Sin cut us off from the source of spiritual life which is God.

Humans are in this terrible condition from conception itself. As David wrote, "...in sin did my mother conceive me" (Ps. 51:5). David confesses here not for his mother, but on his own behalf.

Paul wrote, "...you were dead in your transgressions and sins, in which you used to live when you followed the ways of this world...." This tragic state of being, wrote Paul, was according to the devil "who now works in the sons of disobedience" (Eph. 2:2c).

For this reason, Jesus told Nicodemus that to enter the kingdom of heaven he must be "born again." In other words, Nicodemus had to be delivered from his natural condition of spiritual death to one of spiritual life.

But "how could this be?" wondered Nicodemus. Jesus explained that flesh and blood could never make this spiritual rebirth take place on its own (Jn. 3:3-8). A miraculous act of God's grace was required (Jn. 1:12-13).

As Jesus made clear, this new spiritual life is the *gift*

of God (1 Cor. 2:12; 1 Pet. 1:3-4). A true gift, it's not earned but is made possible by Jesus' dying on the cross in payment for sin.

Receiving the gift of new spiritual life is not some trade or deal whereby a person first repents and God then gives them new birth in return. How can a person who is spiritually dead and in bondage repent? They cannot. Jesus made this point very clear to Nicodemus. Rather, at the moment of faith, God gives new life and with it comes the capacity to repent.

The gift of new spiritual life is also termed repentance which is granted by God (2 Tim. 2:25-26). More than a mere change of mind about God and sorrow for sin, true repentance is to be regenerated and changed by God's power. It's to be given a new nature that hates sin and loves righteousness.

Do we doubt this? How then does our old fallen nature, which can never please God or obey him, ever feel sorrow for sin or think differently about God? Such a thing is impossible. Our old nature remains at enmity with him even after salvation. Like Jesus said, we must first be born again if we are to enter the kingdom of God! We need a new nature!

In raising us to new spiritual life, Jesus calls us out of death to life even as he raised Lazarus from the dead by the sheer power of his word. In this way, God imparts a new nature in us to coexist with our fallen one.

This new nature delights to obey and do God's will. This nature desires to be holy as God is holy. Therefore,

our spiritual rebirth or regeneration is where the process of sanctification begins.

THE HOLY SPIRIT

Regeneration happens by the power of the Holy Spirit.
The third person of the Trinity actively quickens the
spiritually dead person to new spiritual life. From that
moment on, the Spirit of God indwells the believer with
the life of God. This amazing, miraculous event occurs
in a second of time by the same invisible power of God
that raised Jesus from the dead.

At the last supper, Jesus promised his disciples they
would receive the Holy Spirit who would change them
forever. The Spirit would write God's holy laws on their
hearts and empower their minds to understand, love and
obey God.

Paul wrote that without the Holy Spirit it's impossible to be a Christian. God's Spirit makes conversion
possible. His miraculous power changes a life. Conversion is not a matter of saying the right words or having
a feeling. Conversion is a changed life by God's direct
intervention.

Because the Spirit of God is the *Holy* Spirit, his work
in the believer's life is always to produce holiness. He
does this by pointing us to Jesus so we become more
and more like him, and unlike the devil that we followed
in our fallen state. Gradually, God's Spirit works to restore us to godliness. This process is our sanctification.

Though never perfect in this life, we're changed daily

to reflect more of God's image as originally intended before the fall. We wrestle with the world, the flesh and the devil as God would exercise us in godliness and holiness.

To further the process of our sanctification, Paul commands in his letters that we walk in the Spirit and put our old nature to death with all its deeds and desires. Paul calls us to be filled with God's Spirit who produces the fruit of the Spirit in us: love, joy, peace, patience and more; and the gifts of the Spirit to do God's work in the world.

The presence of God's Spirit in our heart also enables us to call God, "Father." Being born again through the Holy Spirit, we've entered into God's spiritual family and have a new relationship with him—one that by his own promise to us is eternal. In this knowledge, we have the hope to endure, that God our Father will help us and keep us through the struggles of our Christian life.

GOOD WORKS

The chief proof of the Holy Spirit's genuine presence in any believer's life is the evidence of *good works*. Jesus taught his disciples that "you will know them by their fruits" (Matt. 7:16).

The point here, however, is not that any people are saved by their own good works or that good works contribute to anyone's salvation. God's standard for salvation "by works" is absolute perfection. No one but Jesus ever fulfilled this standard, because he alone lived a sinless life.

Rather, we're saved "by faith" in Jesus: through the good works and sacrificial death that he offered for us. In producing our own good works thereafter, we simply demonstrate that we've been truly born again and saved by God's grace through faith. At our spiritual rebirth, the Holy Spirit came to dwell in us and he produces "good works" in us through God's supernatural power.

Though these good works do not save us or even contribute to our salvation, they're the sign of a salvation that has already taken place. These good works are the essential evidence that the faith we profess in Christ is a genuine faith from God (Eph. 2:8-10). They confirm that God's Spirit is at work in us doing what we could never do on our own (Phil. 2:12-13).

Without the Holy Spirit's presence in a human life, and without "good works" as the evidence of salvation, the Bible assures us that one was never truly saved. Again, works do not bring salvation, but serve as proof of an existing salvation which is God's gracious work in the believer.

That's why the Apostle James could teach "faith without works is dead" (Jam. 2:20, 26). He meant that a profession of faith without the evidence of good works to corroborate it was not true faith at all. The lack of works in this case was a sign that God through the Holy Spirit was not active and present in a person's life—regardless of what that person might say with their words. Again, as Jesus said, "You will know them by their fruits."

However, when the Holy Spirit indwells a person

his presence results in a changed life that bears good fruit to varying degrees. Such fruit is not a human feat but the gift of God.

For as long as we live, our sanctification continues. It is a life-long process of repentance. The thief on the cross lived only hours after coming to faith in Jesus. Yet, he was changed in that short time. A child coming to salvation changes over a long, full lifetime.

As it is, God has not chosen to make us perfect instantly or in this life. Still, our sanctification produces a real and practical righteousness in our own behavior.

In addition to a practical change in our own behavior, we possess Christ's "perfect righteousness" by faith. It's the righteousness of Christ imputed to us or put to us through our faith in him, according to divine promise.

MEANS OF GRACE

To the Philippians, Paul wrote, "…work out your salvation with fear and trembling; for it is God who works in you…" (Phil. 2:12b-13a). In other words, though sanctification is God's work in us, we're not to remain passive in the process. To the contrary, God calls us to respond actively to his grace. Our active participation proves a genuine and real conversion.

To help us "work out" our salvation, God provides what may be termed practical *means of grace*. The invisible God often uses *means* to accomplish his *ends*. These means are actual things or channels through which God extends grace to us. We grow in our sanctification as we make use of these means. Through the Holy Spirit, these *means of grace* help us develop our spiritual life.

Baptism is one such means of grace. Through the sacrament of baptism, we publicly acknowledge before God and his people our death to sin and resurrection to new spiritual life through faith in Christ. As we go under the water, we're symbolically "buried with Christ" by faith and "raised" as we come up again (Col. 2:12). Water also symbolizes cleansing from sin.

Another of the means of grace is God's Word as recorded in the Old and New Testaments. The Bible contains God's special revelation to us, his inspired truth written down in sixty-six books.

Like Christ himself, the Word made flesh, the scriptures are both human and divine (Jn. 1:14). In reflecting the personalities and styles of the authors who wrote them, they are genuinely human. As originally given through these fallible, human instruments, the scriptures are also divine and without error through the inspiration of the Holy Spirit (2 Tim. 3:16). Peter wrote that no scripture is the product of human effort alone, but was given by inspiration of God (2 Pet. 1:21).

For this reason, the Holy Scriptures provide us with correction, guidance, worship, teaching, history, prophecy and God's precious promises. Their preservation through the millennia, in spite of efforts to destroy them, has been by God's promise and is a further sign of their divinity.

Worship and fellowship with other believers are means of grace essential to spiritual growth as well. Scripture exhorts us to praise God, thank him and worship him, individually and in the company of others—the body of Christ, the church of God. "Not forsaking the assembling of ourselves together…" is a command and admonition of the Lord (Heb. 10:25). We grow in the presence of others as we "spur one another on toward love and good deeds" (Heb. 10:24).

Prayer remains another essential component of our spiritual life. On one hand, prayer is as natural as breathing in air, and on the other, as natural as a child talking to a parent. Yet we easily forget to pray. But we're exhorted to pray always and everywhere, constantly calling upon God in every circumstance and for all things, and to do so with thanksgiving for his blessings.

In praying, we're to trust God and not lose heart, to seek forgiveness, and to intercede for one another and the world. Such prayer reminds us of our communion with God and dependence upon him. And though we often don't know how to pray as we ought, the Holy Spirit intercedes for us in accordance with God's perfect will, and the living Christ intercedes for us at the Father's right hand (Rom. 8:26-27, 34).

At the last supper, Jesus instituted the sacrament of Holy Communion or Holy Eucharist. On the night before he died, he commanded his followers to continue the regular practice of breaking the bread and passing the cup in remembrance of his death and resurrection.

These physical elements are gracious signs of his broken body and blood poured out for our salvation. Participating in this holy ordinance strengthens our faith and communion with Christ.

By making use of the various means of grace God has provided for us, we're enabled to grow in our spiritual lives. Though we slip and fall once and again, God encourages us through these gifts to continue with him on our path to heaven.

Like Christian in Pilgrim's Progress traveling through a difficult and dangerous land, we press on with God's precious promises that, "He who has begun a good work in you will complete it until the day of Jesus Christ" and "lo, I am with you always" (Phil. 1:6; Matt. 28:20b).

THE ARMOR OF GOD

In an ongoing struggle for sanctification, we battle more than with ourselves and the world around us. The one who first tempted our ancient ancestors in the Garden still works.

As Paul reminds us, our fight is not merely with "flesh and blood," but with satanic forces arrayed against us and the devil himself (Eph. 6:12). Our adversary roams about "like a roaring lion, seeking whom he may devour" (1 Pet. 5:8).

Satan and his devils are invisible powers, organized for evil purpose to oppose God and destroy his creatures. As we learn from the scriptures, these evil powers are greater than any human power. There power is so great, even the mighty angel had to battle with the "Prince of Persia" for twenty-one days in attempting to reach Daniel with God's message (Dan. 10:13).

The devil is a real, powerful, personal being. He is the unseen "ruler of the kingdom of the air," who manipulates, tempts, taunts, and opposes human beings. He's a liar, a thief and a murderer. To doubt or deny his existence is utter foolishness.

At the same time, we need to remember that Satan, though powerful and intelligent, is only a creature of God. Great as his powers are, they are limited. God however is infinite, almighty and all-knowing, and the devil trembles at the very mention of his name. Satan exists by God's permission and that only for a season. As the Bible promises, the old devil will be destroyed at the end of time in the Lake of Fire where his punishment will never end (Rev. 20:10).

In the meantime, knowing we have this powerful adversary, God exhorts us in our struggle to depend upon his mighty power, freely offered. For, "He who is in you is greater than he who is in the world" (1 Jn. 4:4b). In other words, Christ who is in us is greater than the devil.

Furthermore, during his earthly life, Jesus resisted the devil when tempted. In the wilderness, Jesus said, "Away from me, Satan! For it is written: 'Worship the Lord your God, and serve him only.'" (Matt. 4:10). Again, in Gethsemane, he resisted Satan as he chose to do God's will that we might be saved. Tempted in every way we are, Jesus was without sin. Now, as we trust in him, he promises a way of escape that we may bear the devil's attack in the evil day (1 Cor. 10:13).

We're also to make use of "the whole armor of God" in our fight with evil powers (Eph. 6:11a). This spiritual armor, described by Paul in his letter to the Ephesians, is patterned after what a mighty Roman soldier wore when dressed in full body armor (Eph. 6:11-20). Properly protected with God's armor, we can stand our ground when the devil attacks in what is a spiritual battle.

The elements of God's armor include: truth, righteousness, the gospel, faith, salvation, the Word of God—a weapon for both offense and defense—and prayer for ourselves, God's people and those who proclaim God's gospel in the world. Because our warfare with Satan is spiritual, so are our weapons. God's weapons are powerful enough to achieve his holy purpose (2 Cor. 10:3-6).

As we resist the devil with God's power and armor, we have this promise in the scriptures that the devil will run away: "Resist the devil, and he will flee from you," (Jam. 4:7b). Powerful as Satan is, he's nonetheless a coward. God's holy power and presence terrify him.

IN THE TWINKLING OF AN EYE

The great hope of all Christians is that our grievous warfare with the world, the flesh and the devil has a victorious end. One day, we'll be delivered permanently from our enemies and changed completely forever.

Until then, God's will is that we continue to do battle

with evil during the rest of our earthly lives. He could have chosen otherwise. But this painful struggle is God's means of perfecting us through the school of suffering and difficulty (Rom. 5:3-4; 1 Pet. 4:1-2). Our struggles wean us from sin as we learn to hate it and love righteousness.

Walking through this life-long process with God, we have his promise of encouragement that "he who endures to the end will be saved." We also have Christ's promise that he'll not lose so much as one of those who turn to him (Jn. 6:39, 10:27-30).

But when we finally see Jesus, the painful work of our sanctification will be complete. For when we see him, we shall be made like him—reflecting the goodness and holiness of our Maker (1 Cor. 13:12; 1 Jn. 3:2). We'll be without a sinful nature, restored to that original state of righteousness lost by our race in the fall, never to lose it again.

When Christ returns, those who've died will be resurrected first, rising "to meet the Lord in the air" (1 Th. 4:17b). Those who are alive will follow, transformed and changed in the twinkling of an eye (1 Cor. 15:51-52).

Death, suffering, loss and evil will be destroyed. The effect of the curse will be utterly removed. Sin will be gone forever. We shall know only righteousness and holiness before the Lord—with joy and eternal happiness that no creature can comprehend or imagine.

None of this is the sentimental wishful thinking of popular culture. None of this is automatic. Our glorious sanctification and the hope of heaven were purchased for us at great price by the Son of God through his holy passion. We receive these gifts by grace through faith.

WHY DID HE DIE:
OUR GLORIFICATION

"And those…he also glorified" Romans 8:30

ON A COOL NOVEMBER NIGHT when I was sixteen, I stood on the edge of a busy four-lane highway by the old ice house and almost took my life. Car lights raced past me in the darkness. What was the point of living, I thought? What I wanted most in life I could never have. I might as well kill myself.

Looking up into the dark night sky at distant stars, I felt numb inside. I had never thought this way before.

For half an hour, I stood there trying to make my decision. Then the thought occurred to me that if I had nothing to live for, I was as good as dead already. If that were true, then why kill myself? I could just continue to live as if I was dead. That way, if I continued to exist, who knows but that something unexpected might happen someday? In the meantime I could live as if I were dead, without caring about anything or anyone. I'd have nothing to lose. So I walked home.

Somehow I had never once thought of God that night. I didn't realize that my life's purpose was to glorify him. I didn't understand that Christ had died to purchase eternity and immortality for me. Conveniently, I'd also forgotten any concept of judgment or hell.

How could I have known then that on another November night—almost thirty years later—God would give me a vision to bring his Word to the world in a new way?

How grateful I am I didn't kill myself that night as a young boy. God preserved my life and prepared me to serve him for these few, fast, fleeting years on earth. He brought me my wife, Betty, to love and to share our lives and mission together. He has blessed me in so many ways.

Now, when my death does come, I'll receive the crown of life that our God graciously promised to those who love him. On that day, all that I once had sought and dreamed about would be loss when compared to living in the presence of Christ who made the universe and died for me.

Who can comprehend these amazing things? When I see Jesus, I'll be made like him! I will dwell in his holy presence to serve and glorify him forever!

I'll rejoice again to see those I've loved, dear family and friends whose names are found written in the Lamb's Book of Life! All wounds will be healed; all pains forgotten.

In that glorious heaven, I'll find our ancient ancestors, Adam and Eve, Abel, Seth and Noah. I'll meet our mighty spiritual kin, Abraham and Sarah, Isaac and Rebecca, Jacob, Moses, David, Mary, Peter and Paul—heroes of the faith—and myriads more, God's great cloud of witnesses throughout all the ages.

Countless numbers will be in this heaven from every tongue and tribe and nation on earth. I'll be there among them—for Christ is in me, the hope of glory! By the grace of my Father and the holy sacrifice of his Son, I will dwell with them in the house of the Lord forever.

———◦◦◦———

Amazingly, the shameful, public execution of the perfect, sinless God-Man secured for believers the prize of their *glorification*. Sinners who deserve eternal "damnation" in God's infinite justice instead receive the extreme opposite in reward for Christ's suffering: glorification. Our redeemed bodies will be elevated to celestial glory with God forever. For everlasting ages, we'll experience eternal splendor and beatific happiness in our Creator's presence and service.

That we might be glorified then with God is a seventh great purpose in the passion of his Son.

PARADISE

In the New Testament, the word "paradise" is used only three times. The ancient origin of the word had to do with the concept of a walled-garden. Later, it referred to gardens such as belonged to the kings of Persia. We're reminded of the original Garden, guarded after the fall by the cherubim with a flaming sword to keep out fallen humanity.

In its most famous usage, Jesus spoke of paradise when he comforted the thief dying on the cross beside him. Jesus promised, "...today you will be with me in paradise" (Lk. 23:43). Paradise is the place where the conscious, living souls of believers go upon the death of their bodies.

The Apostle Paul taught that at death a Christian's soul immediately left the body to be present with the Lord: "to be absent from the body and to be present with the Lord" (2 Cor. 5:8). The soul (the very essence of the human person: "you" will be with "me") continues its existence with the Lord. This takes place in paradise.

As we also learn from Paul, paradise is the "third heaven," a place of unspeakable glory (2 Cor. 12:3-4). Paul was taken there by God in a vision, where he experienced such things as he could not describe.

In this wondrous place, the souls of all believers who've died await the consummation of all things. They wait for that great day when Christ will return and their eternal souls are united with their new bodies, spiritual bodies prepared for everlasting life.

For this reason, Christians are not to mourn and grieve at death as the world does. Death for the Christian is not annihilation of the person, nor is it the prospect of punishment.

Instead, we look forward to eternity with a certain hope that's an anchor for the soul. At death, we go to be with the Lord in paradise until the resurrection.

A PHYSICAL RESURRECTION

Because Christ rose bodily from death, believers that have died are buried in expectation of a physical resurrection like his. The hope of the resurrection means that our souls won't live forever in some vague disembodied state. Nor will we be reincarnated as some other person or creature.

Rather, we're each distinct, eternal individuals, made in God's image possessing our own unique bodies. These bodies will be redeemed through resurrection.

Unlike the Greeks, the Jews held the body in high estimation as a thing good and worthy of respect. The human body had been created by God, and its Maker declared it "good" at creation. However, subjected to death after the fall, the human body, as the vehicle for the commission of sin, suffered the indignity of decay. It returned to dust, just as God promised in the Garden.

But through his death and resurrection, Jesus provided deliverance from death's power and gave us new life and the hope of a bodily resurrection.

Paul taught these great truths to the Corinthians, who were ignorant about the resurrection. At death, he wrote, our body is buried, like a seed planted in the ground. At the resurrection, this "seed" will bear the harvest of a new, redeemed body that's designed and fit for eternal spiritual life with God (1 Cor. 15:35-54).

Upon his resurrection, Jesus was the first fruits of this glorious harvest. His new spiritual body passed through doors, walls and disappeared at will. Yet it was a true body, redeemed from his original body, with real flesh and bones.

Paul taught the Thessalonians when this would occur.

At the trumpet call of God, Christians who had died will be resurrected first. Suddenly, their new bodies will rise physically from the grave by the same creative power that formed Adam from the dust in the first place. At that moment, their eternal souls will be reunited with their new bodies, never to be separated. These resurrected Christians will rise to meet Christ in the air.

Next, those Christians who are alive at Christ's return will follow: changed in the twinkling of an eye and caught up on the clouds to join their Lord. Never will they know death or sin or pain again. They will know only endless joy in the presence of God and the Lamb forever.

This great hope of the resurrection was purchased for us by Jesus Christ at the cross and was demonstrated for us by his own resurrection on the third day. Jesus began the great process of immortality and life. Now we look forward through him to our own resurrection and redemption from eternal death and punishment.

JUDGMENT DAY

The Bible teaches us that death is appointed once for every person, and then comes judgment (Heb. 9:27). On that great and final Judgment Day, each of us must appear before the judgment seat of Christ (2 Cor. 5:10; Rom. 14:10; Acts 17:31). To think therefore that this life on earth is all there is, and that there will be no final accounting, is foolish denial and a great deceit.

For unbelievers, the Day of Judgment will be one

of terror and regret. On that day they will be found guilty and condemned for all eternity without reprieve or escape. Those who had God's Law will be judged by God's Law. Those who did not have the Law will be judged by the light of conscience and God's laws written in their hearts.

Because no one has lived up to these standards, all fall short, but only those without Christ will be lost (Rom. 3:9-20). Their final condemnation was assured even while they lived (Jn. 3:18).

With perfect justice, God will hold the lost accountable for every thought, word and deed of their lives. For them, this day is for their sentencing. Souls rejoined to their bodies, the lost will be condemned and delivered to everlasting destruction and punishment with the devil and his angels in the Lake of Fire (Rev. 20:11-15). They will be removed from all love, grace, hope and goodness forever.

Eternal condemnation and punishment is what all humans deserve and, apart from Christ, is what we all would receive. But thanks be to God that he has given us his Son to save us!

For believers, Judgment Day will be no day of terror and regret. Believers will all appear before the Lord Jesus. But for us, our appearance before the Lord will be for acquittal of all crimes committed against God and conscience.

Christ already paid our debt by his blood and bore the penalty we deserved. God's court will find us not guilty and will declare us innocent of all charges.

Though we merited eternal condemnation, as believers in Christ, we will escape all penalty, punishment and wrath. No suffering of eternal torments awaits us. Justified by faith in Christ, we will receive the reward of eternal life instead.

Having been delivered by Christ from all peril and judgment, nothing but boundless bliss and eternal, inexpressible joy awaits the redeemed and reconciled children of God.

NEW HEAVEN AND EARTH

Condemned to futility and death, the entire creation has groaned for redemption ever since the fall. Under God's curse, the creation has longed eagerly for the day of his new creation.

But on that great day of God, the whole universe will first melt and pass away (2 Pet. 3:10-12). The vast expanse of nearly endless galaxies, solar systems, stars and planets and all their substance, the earth and the heavens, will suddenly collapse upon themselves in one big, fiery, incomprehensible cosmic "bang" comprised of all matter and energy in the universe.

No mere theory, this is a Big Bang "Prophecy" about the destruction of our universe foretold by God's inspired servants for thousands of years. The Psalmist declared this truth in the Old Testament (Ps. 102:26). Isaiah prophesied it 700 years before Christ (Is. 34:4, 65:17). The Apostle Peter foretold this explosive event in the New Testament. The Apostle John proclaimed it in the Book of Revelation (Rev. 6:13-14, 20:11). It will happen!

As Colossians tells us, Christ is the one who "holds all things together" (Col. 1:17). In God's big bang, he simply lets go of all the atoms and order in the universe that he now "holds together." Mankind's atomic explosions, having demonstrated the principles involved, are mere child's play compared to unleashing the stored energy of all the matter in the universe in a single split second.

But this catastrophic explosion is not the end! Nor is it ultimately an expression of God's wrath. From these things, the Lord has promised to create a new heaven and a new earth where only righteousness will dwell. By this cosmic explosion, God acts for the redemption of the universe.

Science again discerns the underlying principles. In the natural realm, matter and energy can be neither created nor destroyed, merely changed from one form to the other. Respecting the laws of his own creation, God can redeem the incredible energy unleashed by an exploding universe to form a new universe, free from the mar of sin.

Here then, in this holy, majestic, new heaven and earth all the redeemed will dwell. All the redeemed who have ever lived from the time of Adam will be there, with Christ who paid the ransom for their release.

GOD AND THE LAMB

On this new earth, God has promised a New Jerusalem, a heavenly city made without human hands. Coming down from heaven, this city will be the dwelling place of God and the redeemed.

Abraham and all the prophets looked forward to this amazing city (Heb. 11:8-10). John described that day in his heavenly vision on Patmos Island (Rev. 21:2-4). He saw a great and majestic city of God appearing upon a glorious new earth.

At the center of the holy city of New Jerusalem will dwell both God our Father and the Lamb who is the Lord Jesus Christ. In this glorious place, there is no temple for they are its temple. There is no sun for they are its light (Is. 60:19; Rev. 21:23). There is no darkness, only eternal day. There is no curse for there is no sin.

As God promised Abraham, the redeemed will be here representing all the "families of the earth." They were blessed through his seed who is Christ. "They have washed their robes in the blood of the Lamb and have made them white" (Rev. 7:14b).

Here in this holy, heavenly city, the redeemed of the Lord will rejoice forever in their Creator and Redeemer with perfect happiness. They'll serve them with absolute obedience and delight.

"No eye has seen, no ear has heard, no mind has conceived what God has prepared for those who love him," wrote the Apostle (1 Cor. 2:9). Fallen creatures in a fallen creation, locked in time and space as we are, the things of heaven are inconceivable to us. Consider the greatest beauty and joy and pleasures in life, and we still have no concept of our immortal existence in the presence of our infinite, holy, majestic God. We see as through a glass darkly (1 Cor. 13:12).

But in heaven our new spiritual bodies will be equipped to enjoy this holy place. Heirs of Christ, we will delight in all that our Creator has so richly prepared for us. Glorious things are spoken of this city of God!

But above all, we will enjoy God and the Lamb themselves, to worship and serve forever as we were created to do before the fall. Here, with the mighty host of angels and all the redeemed, we'll sing with everlasting joy of the glory of our King, who is King of kings and Lord of lords and of his mighty kingdom. In God's presence there is joy and at his right hand there are "pleasures for evermore" (Ps. 16:11).

THE TREE OF LIFE

Just as the story of our race began with the Tree of Life, so it ends with the Tree of Life in God's heavenly city. In heaven, the Tree of Life that was lost is restored to God's people. Each month it bears immortal fruit, and its leaves are for the spiritual healing of the nations (Rev. 22:2).

Adam and Eve were kept from this fruit by the cherubim with a fiery sword, lest they eat and live forever in their sin. But when sin is dead, the redeemed will no longer be excluded from this tree of everlasting life. We'll have complete access to this provision of God.

Eating the fruit of eternity from this tree, we'll forget the sufferings and losses of our earthly lives. With

never-ending thanksgiving, we'll reflect on this unde-
served salvation won for us by Christ who loved us and
gave himself for us.

Eating from the Tree of Life, we'll remember that
the fall of our race took place with the eating of fruit
from a forbidden tree in Eden's garden. Yet, God promised even then to send one to deliver us. Redemption
took place with the sacrifice of his Son on a tree outside
Jerusalem.

For Christ humbled himself for a season, to be
beaten, rejected and die upon the cross, that by his bloody
passion, he might accomplish God's great and mighty
purposes—to purchase a people for himself, to enjoy his
glory and goodness forever through endless ages everlasting.

Unto the Lamb belong all glory and honor and praise
forever! Amen.

Finishing the Race

In his letter to the Hebrews, the New Testament writer
exhorts God's people to complete the race before them:
"…and let us run with perseverance the race marked out
for us" (Heb. 12:1).

This race before us is our journey to heaven. Heaven
is its finish line. When tempted by the difficulties of our
Christian life to quit this race, we're called to remember
the goal.

Greek athletes trained for great endurance in prepara-
tion for their famous Olympic competitions. They under-

went this difficult training to win prizes that were passing away, mere garlands or a wreath, and the passing adulation of the world. Today no one remembers their names.

But the race of the Christian life has an eternal destination and an everlasting prize. Jesus, we're told, awaits us at the finish line. When Satan, sin and death seek to discourage us to fall away, we're to look to Jesus for strength and perseverance as we run. He endured the passion!

God reminds us that we're also surrounded by a great cloud of witnesses who've gone before (Heb. 12:1). They've run this race. They've crossed the line. They'll receive the crown of everlasting life on the great Day of Judgment. And they await the outcome of our race.

So let us run, remembering that "The one who calls you is faithful and *he* will do it" (1 Th. 5:24). In trust and hope, let's run our race by God's power and grace. He calls us to it.

For God's holy purpose is to bring to his kingdom everyone whose name was written in the Lamb's Book of Life before the foundation of the world. None can take them from his hand.

Strengthening weak knees, let's continue our race to its glorious destination—recalling the great purposes of God in the passion of his Son: nothing less than the redemption of the world through our Lord Jesus Christ! "For God so loved the world, that he gave his only begotten Son, that whosoever believeth in him should not perish, but have everlasting life" (Jn. 3:16).

Victors will receive the Crown of Life!

———◦◦◦———

A PRAYER OF REPENTANCE AND FAITH

Heavenly Father, I confess that I've sinned against you in my thoughts, words and deeds, and that I deserve your judgment. But I believe that Jesus Christ died for my sins on the cross at Calvary and rose again from the dead. Forgive my sins in his name, I pray. Save me and change me by your grace that I may do your will. I pray for your mercy upon me and all those who trust in you. I praise you and thank you for the passion of Jesus Christ your Son.

- Thank you for your promise to send a Savior to die for me
- Thank you that Jesus died to appease your holy anger
- Thank you for redeeming me from bondage to Satan, sin and death
- Thank you for justifying me before you by faith
- Thank you for reconciling me to you through Christ
- Thank you for your promise to sanctify me through your Holy Spirit
- Thank you for your promise to glorify me with you in heaven forever

In Jesus' name. Amen.